Be the One

Be the One

Six True Stories of
Teens Overcoming
Hardship with Hope

BYRON PITTS

SIMON & SCHUSTER BFYR

NEW YORK   LONDON   TORONTO   SYDNEY   NEW DELHI

Note to the reader:
Certain names and other characteristics have been changed.

SIMON & SCHUSTER BFYR

An imprint of Simon & Schuster Children's Publishing Division
1230 Avenue of the Americas, New York, New York 10020
SIMON & SCHUSTER BFYR is a trademark of Simon & Schuster, Inc.
For information about special discounts for bulk purchases, please contact
Simon & Schuster Special Sales at 1-866-506-1949 or
business@simonandschuster.com.
The Simon & Schuster Speakers Bureau can bring authors to your live event.
For more information or to book an event, contact
the Simon & Schuster Speakers Bureau at 1-866-248-3049 or
visit our website at www.simonspeakers.com.
Jacket design by Chloë Foglia
Interior design by Hilary Zarycky
The text for this book was set in Sabon.
Manufactured in the United States of America
4 6 8 10 9 7 5
CIP data for this book is available from the Library of Congress.
ISBN 978-1-4424-8382-8
ISBN 978-1-4424-8384-2 (eBook)

To the members of the Horatio Alger Association, men and women who've committed their time and treasure to help the next generation. Association members are some of the most accomplished people in the United States and Canada. Many have overcome some of the most challenging circumstances one can imagine. Like the young people in this book, there is a toughness to each of them and an endless optimism about life and what's possible to those who dream and work.

INTRODUCTION

hen I was a boy, my grandmother would always greet me with the sweetest touch and kindest words. She'd give me a big hug, pull me close, and whisper in my ear, "You're the one." No matter what was going on in my life, everything felt better when I heard her voice and those words washed over me. For the longest time I thought her greeting meant I was somehow special. Back then I wore glasses and was toothpick thin. I had a head that I hadn't grown into yet and a noticeable stutter. So any suggestion I was special in a good way certainly meant something to me.

But as I got older, I came to realize "You're the one" meant something else. She was encouraging me to be okay with who I was, to believe in who I'd become, and to be the one (with God's loving grace) to choose a positive path.

I came to that conclusion after meeting a diverse group of young people with challenges far greater than mine who had somehow chosen on their own to be the one to take a better path for themselves. They'd realized they had a role to play in changing their circumstances.

How do you explain it, young people who face what seem like insurmountable odds and yet succeed? Is it something with which they were born? Did the right influences come into their lives at the right time? Luck? Grace? Or is it a miracle?

I believe it is all those things but something more. That more is . . . the individual, the person who makes the choice to change oneself and even one's circumstances when possible, the person who embraces hope over heartache no matter the situation. Many of us know people like this but fail to realize that that very person may live inside each of us: a tiger ready to leap out and change the world. Healing can come from many places, but it starts and ends with you, the individual who finds the hero inside your own heart. Luck has been described as what happens when preparation and location meet; grace, as unmerited gifts from God; and a miracle, as an extraordinary event that surpasses human understanding. I certainly believe in the supernatural power of God, but there is an African proverb that states: "When you pray, move your feet." This is a book about young people who move their feet.

Inside these pages are the real stories of real preteens and young adults who have overcome challenges of many kinds: poverty, family mental illness, abandonment, obesity, neglect, war, homelessness, violence, molestation, and bullying. None would describe themselves as special or possessing any unique gifts. On many levels they are what you would describe as remarkably ordinary. All would agree that at an early age they were dealt a bad hand. And they played it with little or no complaint and often with little help. They were able to "be the one" for themselves because they had to be. There was no plan B. No one was coming quickly to rescue them, so they chose to rescue themselves.

As a journalist for more than thirty years, I have seen courage and cowardice in most of their forms. I have witnessed the powerful and the powerless in action. Many have names history will recall. Most do not. But few, if any, have inspired me more than the people you are about to meet. Most of them showed courage when no one was looking, displayed wisdom beyond their years. Each in his or her own way possesses an earnest and joyful spirit that defies his or her circumstances. For some that optimism seems to come more easily. For all it was a choice. And each can teach us something about taking personal responsibility for our lot in life. These are not bootstrap stories of young people who made it on their own. But rather, young people who endured when they had to, sought out others when they could, and managed to stay faithful to their dreams and ambitions when they could very easily have given up. More than survivors, they are overcomers.

Over the years I've spent considerable time with

grade school, high school, and college students . . . people at every rung of the academic and social ladders. And I noticed a pattern: Regardless of their standing, so many of them were hurting, unsure and often even fearful about their own future. Sometimes this fear bordered on paralysis. They were stuck. As if the world had already dictated their future and they were simply innocent bystanders. The people you're about to meet decided early on that they would not be bystanders.

"Hero" is a word we use too often in our culture. An accolade usually heaped upon athletes and celebrities. But people who defend life and save lives deserve such titles. Well, the kids in this book all saved at least one life: their own.

That's why they are my heroes.

The hero who most inspired this book was an eleven-year-old girl I met at a charter school in a big US city. Her name is Tania Parker. Soon after meeting her, I wanted the world to know her story. And I wanted others who might see some of Tania in their own stories to know they are not alone and to know that heroes come in all sizes and all ages.

Years after we first met, when I reconnected with Tania, I told her she was my hero. She blushed with embarrassment. "Me?!" she giggled.

Yes, Tania Parker is my hero because the life she lives, and a question she asked me about her plight, are both heartbreaking and inspiring.

I met Tania at a school assembly when she was eleven. I was there to talk to her entire school about the importance of education and working hard. At the end of my remarks Tania walked up to me and asked the following question: "Mr. Pitts, when you were my age, where did you go, where did you hide, when the world hurt too much?"

She took my breath away.

The people you're about to meet have all asked a similar question in their own lives. They each found an answer. This book chronicles their journeys to those answers.

They all chose to be the one to help turn around their own lives. And some have made part of their life's work be to inspire and encourage others. To be the one to stand up for those not yet ready to stand up for themselves.

TANIA

"No one loved me. So I learned to love myself."

For Tania a hard lesson in rejection came at the age of four.

"I won't be seeing you again."

Those were the last six words Tania ever heard from her birth mother. That's it. Six words. Almost every day thereafter she'd repeat them to herself, and in time she'd write them down. We're all shaped in some way by the smallest of memories from our earliest recollections of life. Sometimes it's a scar we picked up on the playground. For Tania it was a scar placed upon her heart by her own mother's words. Tania's mom, Mary Johnson, had a new boyfriend and a new baby. There was no room in her life for her firstborn. The boyfriend gave Mary a choice: that child or him.

She chose him.

Mary was little more than a teenager herself. She'd had Tania when she was sixteen, and she was a stranger to anything that resembled stability: drugs, violence, and abuse had all been part of her life. The new boyfriend offered her the chance at a fresh start, and that meant Tania was now the state's full-time responsibility.

Child protective services already had a long file on Tania. After her birth mother no longer had any use for her (Mary would reappear periodically—not to see Tania, but to mooch off of the goodwill of whoever was caring for her), Tania moved several times over the next few years, from one relative's house to the next. Sometimes she would share a bed with a cousin or snuggle alone on a couch or the floor. Even before she'd learned to read or write, her soul understood hardship. Tania had been known to "the system" almost from birth. She had already been in and out of foster care, most often cared for by a foster mother named Gladys Dundalk. Gladys was in her mid-sixties, with two adult children and three grandchildren of her own.

So by the time Tania's mother formally rejected her, making her a ward of the state, Gladys took Tania by the hand and they headed home to a two-story shoe box of a house in a rough section of the city. This would prove to be a mutually beneficial arrangement. Tania would gain what looked like stability and safety. Gladys would get a monthly check from the state and a suitable caregiver/companion when her diabetes and fainting spells worsened. In poker terms, this was not a royal flush for Tania, but it was better than the hand she had been born with. And like any good poker player, this now six-year-old girl knew to play the hand she held, not the one she wanted.

Forty years before Tania was born, the area was a thriving, working-class African American neighborhood. It was in one of the old industrial cities in the east where most men made their living in manufacturing or construction, and women worked in factories or stayed at home. Neither time nor the crack epidemic of the early 1980s have been kind to the community. Today men out of work spend much of the day peering out windows, sitting on porches, or standing on street corners. Countless heroin clinics now occupy space that once housed small businesses and churches. Drug deals take place in broad daylight. In a neighborhood that once thrived with small family-owned shops and was supported by wage earners from local factories and the shipyards, the biggest employers on the block now are the dealers. According to the Drug Enforcement Administration, every "drug corner" could have twenty to thirty thousand dollars in cash tucked behind the bricks of an abandoned building, many of which litter the neighborhood. But it is the place Tania still calls home . . . and a place that—at the time, at least—held the promise of love when Gladys officially adopted her.

There is an African proverb: "It takes a village to raise a child." In many ways the tribe Tania was born to abandoned her, and so it was left to her to build her own. The comfort of a "village" would elude her for some time.

"Every day I would sit at the top of the stairs and wait for my momma to pick me up." From age four to age ten Tania held on to hope that her birth mother would walk through the front door and rescue her. So for six years she would pass a few hours each day sitting at the top of a narrow staircase, staring down at the front door, waiting for a visitor who would never arrive.

Whether it was blind optimism or childhood naivety, it ended. At age ten she abruptly stopped waiting at the top of the staircase for her mother's return. Instead of her mom coming to rescue her, a new foster kid was added to the family. He would turn her already challenging life into a living hell.

"It all changed when he moved in. I came home from school one day and there he was. He was sixteen years old . . . big for his age. For some reason he scared me the moment I laid eyes on him."

Shy by nature, Tania could muster up only a nod to her new "family member," and he seemed to take no particular interest in her. Tania's foster mom seemed mostly indifferent; he was another mouth to feed and additional money from the state. "He will only be here temporarily," Gladys told Tania. It proved to be long enough.

"He raped me the first night." Tears still well in her eyes anytime the subject of Anthony or the abuse is raised. Her words are vague. Her thousand-yard stare is full of dark and painful details. "He would usually come in my room after Momma was asleep." (Tania grew to see her foster mother as her real mom or at least the adult who behaved closest to how a loving parent might.) "The first night he woke me from a sound sleep. I felt his hand over my mouth. He'd say the same thing every time. 'This is our secret. Don't tell anyone. No one will believe you. No one will care.'"

Being abandoned by her mother had been a slow and numbing pain. Coping with it had proved to be instructional. "Whenever I got sad or started missing my mother, I'd think about one of the characters in one of my books or in the Bible stories I'd learn in Sunday school. There's always a happy ending." It was that ability to get lost in the characters of her favorite books that now helped Tania block out the physical pain if not the psychological injury of her sexual abuse. Her grades began to slip in school. She became even more introverted. But no one seemed to take notice. So her soul and her psyche waited for her happy ending.

"Many of my teachers in grade school always called me an 'old soul.' I was never really sure what it meant, but I took it as a compliment. I did all the things kids my age do, but I knew I had to look out for myself. I loved school. Hated my life at home, so my safe place became books. I decided Harry Potter was me and I was Harry Potter. We'd both been separated from our parents. We both had to survive scary experiences. When I was in middle school, the scariest part of my day was going home."

Having been diagnosed with attention deficit disorder (ADD) in third grade, Tania had been placed in remedial math and reading classes for years. She hated it. Tania spent much of her energy trying to fit in at school, striving to be average, to be normal, and to go mostly unnoticed. For her, remedial classes screamed, *NOT normal*. She was teased mercilessly. Few boys talked to her, and countless girls either bullied or ignored her. She was never certain which hurt more, ridicule or rejection. So she mostly kept to herself. Her smile became her shield. No one would know the hurt behind it . . . the pain in school, the abandonment and abuse at home.

Despite it all, Tania always remained confident enough to ask questions. She asked questions in class, in the cafeteria, and at home. Tania felt ashamed of so many things in her life, but she had never lost her desire to learn more. It was less a sense of curiosity and more a longing to improve her place in the world. Early on, Tania figured out life was often unfair. She could let herself drown or find a way out. Asking questions became her rope. If she had a question, she would ask it. Except when it came to her molester. She never talked about it, to anyone. But one day in school her rope became handy.

Like most schools, Tania's held frequent assemblies. One in particular struck a chord. The school invited a local celebrity who'd written a book about the importance of family and faith. Tania thought it seemed somewhat relatable: She longed for her own family and enjoyed the way her church made her feel. And if that constituted faith, hers was strong. Like almost every other public speaker at school, he talked about the importance of education, hard work, and a positive attitude. Yet he also talked about some of his hardships, like being abandoned by his father as a boy and not liking himself. Now he was talking Tania's language. This was the first time she had ever heard an adult talking about painful moments from when he or she was young. It looked like his life had reached a happy ending. So by the time his talk was over, Tania thought, *Why not?* Why not ask him how he survived bad times?

Tania waited until classmates, teachers, and staff members had asked their questions. The line had probably been about thirty people deep. Tania was the last in line. By now most had clustered into small groups around the room, waiting for the assembly to formally end. The guest speaker was no longer the center of attention in the room. So the moment was right. It was as if Tania and the visitor were standing together alone. She wanted to make sure no one at school could hear what she had to say. "I was nervous, so I wrote the question on a piece of paper." When she had the visitor's attention, Tania cleared her throat, looked up over her glasses, and asked: "Mr. Pitts, when you were my age, where did you go, where did you hide, when the world hurt too much?" He seemed stunned by the question. Tania was surprised she'd actually found the courage and the words to ask. For several moments they just looked at each other. *Did he hear my question?* she wondered. Indeed he had.

"I hide in my faith," he said. "There are angels on earth. You don't have to go looking for them, they will find you. Just hold on."

Hold on to what? she wondered. But she was grateful he'd listened and seemed sincere. Tania had found many points in life when there was power in someone listening, in being heard. The visitor asked permission from Tania's teacher to leave his business card so the two could correspond. It was a good day. Tania had gotten an answer to her question and a pen pal. The two would write to each other for years to come.

That visitor was me. It was a life-changing encounter. For both of us, really. Tania's question planted the seed for this book. Most of us ask that very same or a similar question in life. Tania is fighting courageously hard to find the answer for her life.

We remain pen pals. She's kept that first letter inside her nightstand with a small photo album filled with pictures of her mother and sister. It took great courage for Tania to reveal her hurt to a stranger. Somewhere, somehow, she's always had good instincts about people. She instantly knew her foster brother was trouble. She could pick out friend or foe the first day of school in the fall. She knew her foster mother had limitations but that her heart was in the right place. She knew there was some truth for her because faith mattered to her. She didn't know it at the time, but by boldly asking a question, she would change the trajectory of her life. We all need help. The wise among us know to ask for it. I brought Tania's question to the attention of her teacher and counselor. The school conducted its own investigation, and soon Tania's foster brother was moved out. Tania still sleeps in the same bedroom and the same bed she was raped in. She continues to have nightmares. "The nightmares still bother me," she says, "but they can't defeat me."

After she finished middle school, a number of good and caring adults had come into her life. The Smith sisters at her church. Twins, they were also schoolteachers in the public school system. Tania met them at the church she attended with her foster mother. "They were like big sisters to me. They'd take me shopping, out for meals, and occasionally to the hairdresser. I felt like a grown-up. There was also a deacon at our church, Deacon Johnson, who became like a father. Our church had a yearly father-daughter dinner. Deacon Johnson invited me to go with him one year and has taken me ever since. The Smith sisters make sure I have a nice dress to wear, and Deacon Johnson treats me like his own child, even though he has adult children."

By the time she was ready for high school, Tania had survived sexual abuse and her grades had stabilized. She'd already learned many hard lessons in life, and one was the ability to compartmentalize.

"I'm proud to say I'm a survivor. High school meant new friends, new teachers, and new opportunities. No one would know my past or me. It would be a fresh start."

Based on her foster mother's income and neighborhood, Tania was assigned to one of the toughest public high schools in the city. But Tania knew of a private school also in her neighborhood, and with the help of her foster mom and the support of others, she applied and *got in*! It was an all-girls Catholic school that had long been an oasis in a barren land. The daughters of Italian and Irish immigrants had attended the school, and it had been their gateway to college, the middle class, and beyond. African American and Hispanic teenage girls were now taking the same path.

"I've never had a birthday party or a big Christmas, but getting that acceptance letter was like two great holidays combined. I screamed. I think I scared Momma. When I shared the news with her, she gave me a big hug. That night we had my favorite meal. I was on top of the world."

From the very first day of school Tania was assigned a platoon of tutors, and a mentor from the upper grades. In perhaps a sign that fate had turned in her favor, a group of alumni and friends of the school created a fund to cover some cost for students like

Tania. Proof positive perhaps of the saying "The harder you work, the luckier you get." Tania had defied her circumstances—who knew there'd be people waiting to help her?

But even good fortune comes at a price. This was the most demanding academic and social environment Tania had ever been in, from a strict dress code to nightly homework in every class. In her old public school, by simply paying attention and putting in some work, Tania could outperform at least some of her classmates. That wouldn't cut it at this school. Hard circumstance, though, had made her a willing participant when it came to hard work. She looked for the positives everyplace she could.

"The nuns were nice but strict. And most of the girls were cool. The school was much more diverse than my middle or grade school. Black girls, white girls, Hispanic girls, and Asian girls. We were our own United Nations. Test scores showed I was strong in reading and verbal skills. My math scores were awful. But the sisters said with hard work math would get better and I could go to college. College! College?! I know my mother never went to college. I don't know my father, but I doubt he went. I would be the first person in my family to go to college. Wow."

Up until now most of the good moments in Tania's life had come in the pages of her favorite books. Now suddenly good moments were occurring in her day-to-day. For once she felt Harry Potter had nothing on her. Well, maybe only a little bit.

Tania struggled academically her freshman year. She did better her sophomore year. But her junior year was a complete disaster.

Optimism, big dreams, and a modest support system were not enough to fill the potholes that threatened to swallow up Tania. The emotional scars of abandonment and physical and emotional abuses were showing. By the fall of her junior year in high school Tania was becoming a discipline problem. She was suspended for being disruptive in school and disrespectful of authority. The school could provide nurturing, some measure of discipline, and a strong academic foundation, but it lacked the social services resources to provide someone like Tania all that she needed.

Tania's emotional challenges and the school's limitations clashed violently just before Christmas break. "We had a mandatory assembly and I didn't want to go, so I went to the library instead. My teacher insisted I go with the class, and she grabbed my arm. I think I blacked out. I honestly don't remember what happened next, but according to my teacher in her formal complaint, I pushed her. Girls at my school don't push teachers. Since I was already on probation from an earlier suspension, the headmistress said she had no choice but to expel me. I guess I had my chance and I blew it."

Unbeknownst to Tania and her foster mother, one of her old school counselors advocated for an alternative private school for her to attend. After the initial anger, hurt, and embarrassment over her expulsion Tania was in the midst of a comeback.

"My friend Harry Potter has had plenty of close calls. Just when it seemed the worst was about to happen, Harry would figure it out or a miracle would happen. I'm praying for the smarts or the miracle."

It was Tania as an eleven-year-old who posed the central question raised in this book: Where do you go, where do you hide, when the world hurts too much? She gives her own answer now.

"I go to a place where no one can touch me: my imagination. That's why I love books like Harry Potter and *The Hunger Games* so much. Kids as young as me or not much older than me facing difficult odds. During the worst experiences of my life I imagined I was Harry off on an adventure. So no matter the physical or emotional pain I might be experiencing, my soul was safe—off on an adventure. Unlike people in my life, my imagination stays with me—good days and bad."

Despite her expulsion, the people supporting Tania still believed she could make it to college. While she was at the Catholic school, her love of reading grew beyond fiction to works by Langston Hughes. Paraphrasing his poem "Still Here," she says, "I've been torn and I've been battered. My hopes the wind done shattered. Snow done freezed me. Sun done baked me. But I don't care. I'm still here." Tania still believes.

Where do you go, where do you hide, when the world hurts too much? For Tania the answer is: "Where no

one can touch me: my imagination." In the darkest of
moments, Tania says, she has always felt safe in the
deepest reaches of her imagination. That helps explain
her love of fiction. Her imagination guards her still.
Tania doesn't quite have a village, more like a short
assembly line of "angels" who all play valuable roles in
her life. She spends very little time on what she doesn't
have, instead focusing on what she does: adults who
care and a growing confidence that her life will indeed
have a happy ending.

Tania graduated high school. In the fall of 2016 she
started college. Did Harry Potter make it to college?

MASON

"I'm still striving for my goals of success."

Hey, fat boy!" With a whispered sneer and a laugh, the third grader shoved his elbow into the side of his quieter classmate, keeping one eye on the teacher to make sure she did not notice.

Another push, and the weaker kid fell over onto the floor. The bully shoved a notebook and a few papers on top of him. The noise caught the teacher's attention, and she warned the boys at the table in the middle of her class of twenty-five to behave.

With tears burning in his eyes, the child climbed back into his seat as his tormenter leaned in to his ear. "Jelly roll!"

When the clock finally turned to the lunch hour, Mason Harvey asked for permission to go to the nurse's office. The teacher consented, as she did nearly every day when he asked. Mason claimed he had a stomachache. He wanted to call his parents and beg them to pick him up. Of course, he was not really sick. But he was dying inside.

What's that old cliché? "Fat and happy"? Only half of it would describe eight-year-old Mason Harvey. At four feet eight inches tall and 206 pounds, he had a bright smile, but beneath his girth was a boy in pain.

"They'd call me jelly roll, tub-a-loo, chubby roll. Things that didn't make me feel right on the inside. I hated it. And I wanted to punch them."

Chubby-cheeked, with a regulation crew cut and sparkling blue eyes, Mason Harvey from Guthrie, Oklahoma, was a beloved middle child with two brothers, doting parents, and a neighborhood full of extended family. Life was sweet and easy.

His obesity had never really been an issue until third grade, when he was assigned to share a classroom table with his tormenters. The same two boys would taunt and shove and humiliate Mason for three long years.

In the beginning of third grade Mason loved school and worked hard. "I was a straight A student. Super-intendent's honor roll a lot. I've always been an A and B student. First and second grade were definitely straight As."

But soon the morning ride to elementary school became an anticipation of torture. The walk down the halls felt like passing through the gauntlet on the way to execution. The bullies would meet Mason at his locker most mornings or wait impatiently for him at the table they shared in class. They had a routine.

"They'd push me . . . throw things at me. Flick me with their fingers. Usually in the back of the head or the shoulder. They'd take my stuff and throw it on the ground and scatter it everywhere."

Five days a week, seven hours a day, this went on. "It hurt my feelings a lot." It happened in class, the cafeteria, and the hallways. But the worst treatment was reserved for the playground when there was not as many adults around.

His friends would try to protect him, pleading, "Why don't you leave him alone?" The bullies would usually just stare the other kids down or spit a threat in their direction. Mason's friends would eventually back off.

On a crowded playground Mason Harvey often felt alone. "That's why I kinda secluded myself away from everything and focused on my schoolwork, because I felt like an outsider. I didn't feel like I fit in because of all the names that I got called."

As things in third grade got worse, he would make the call home from school nearly every day, complaining of severe stomach pain, nausea, migraines. Whatever ailment would get his parents to school fastest to pick him up. It usually worked. Mom or Dad would rush from work and take their ailing son home, and on occasion to the doctor. This routine went on for weeks. Doctors couldn't explain the problem, so it became cheaper just to stock the medicine cabinet with stomach remedies, pain relievers, and cold suppressants.

When his parents finally began suspecting Mason was making up stories, they continued taking his panicked phone calls but insisted he stay in school. Mason had long ago lost credibility at the nurse's office, and eventually he was reduced to hysterical crying fits in class. His teacher would either send or escort him to a storage room at the back of class until he could regain his composure.

"I hated my life and I hated school," a frustrated Mason says. At the time almost no one really understood the depth of Mason's misery. Not his parents, grandparents, siblings, teachers, not even his closest friends.

Guthrie is a small town of about ten thousand people, around thirty miles north of the capital, Oklahoma City. It is a place where folks know their neighbors. And in no neighborhood in Guthrie was that more true than in Mason's. He lived on a wide swath of family land where almost every neighbor within walking distance or a short drive was a relative. For any school activity or Little League game the Harveys would show up en masse. If his parents could not make an after-school assembly because of work, Mason's grandma or grandpa would certainly be in attendance.

On weekends Mason could walk from home to his grandparents' house during the commercial break of his favorite Saturday-morning cartoon and arrive before the show resumed. And always nearby were his two brothers. The Harvey brothers were born four years apart, Brennan the oldest, Casey the youngest. And Mason is the middle boy. Despite their range in age, the boys always enjoyed one another's company and were fiercely competitive and loyal. Who could jump highest on the trampoline in the backyard? Who could run the fastest to the mailbox? Every competition was weighted, of course, according to age and size. For the Harvey boys, the only thing that mattered more than winning was fairness.

Mason's parents were childhood sweethearts. Home was heaven. Actually, when all his troubles at school started, home became the only place he could hide. There Mason also found comfort in food. After a stressful day at school he would eat three full-size bags of potato chips the moment he got home. Ice cream or doughnuts were a favorite snack as he sat down to do his homework. This was all before his parents got home from work.

Dinnertime was a favorite family ritual in the Harvey household. It was a revered time when television, the workday, playtime, and sports practice were all put on pause so the family could fellowship. Meals consisted of a meat, a vegetable, and a starch. The meals were varied, but the presentation was pretty consistent. The meat was fried. The vegetables were soaked and cooked in animal fat. Butter was plentiful and smeared on bread like icing on a cupcake. And on the days when time did not allow for a home-cooked meal, pizza or fast food was the preferred substitute. For Mason's parents, the home-cooked meals were just like the ones they had enjoyed as children, and they viewed the pizza and fast food as pleasant treats for the children and a small luxury on their modest budget.

After dinner there was always a late-night snack. "Food made me feel better," Mason says. But the worse the bullying got, the more he ate.

Mason's parents were perhaps partly in the dark and

partly in denial about his reasons for overeating and his troubles at school. Every morning after breakfast his mom or dad would drive Mason and his brothers to school. The Harveys are a friendly, talkative bunch. The ride to school was often filled with laughter, family gossip, and whoever was in the driver's seat preaching the virtues of education. No one noticed Mason rolling his eyes in the back when talk turned to school.

But soon his academic performance began to slip, from all As to a few Bs. He was still a good student, but the bullying was a distraction. When given an assignment in class, Mason would focus as hard as he could. It was a great way to block out the bullies. But they were relentless, and at every opportunity they dug into Mason.

"Hey, chubby roll! Fat boy! Fat boy! Fat boy!" At times it sounded like chants at a baseball game. Even though Mason felt alone, he knew he wasn't the only one who had to deal with this kind of thing. He remembered there had been a story on the news about a guy around Mason's age who'd committed suicide. He'd been bullied so badly he killed himself. Mason's parents talked about it some at the dinner table.

"What a shame," his father said with fallen eyes and a slow, sad shake of the head.

"Didn't anyone see the signs?" his mother wondered aloud.

Mason listened. He felt sadness for the boy, but he couldn't relate. Even in his lowest hours Mason never once considered suicide. He couldn't hurt his parents or his brothers like that. But the story on the news did help prompt Mason to finally say something to his parents.

"Hey, Dad, can we talk?" is about as far as Mason got before his tears began to fall. As was his custom, Michael Harvey greeted his son's sadness with an understanding smile and a strong embrace. Mason was breathless and as tense as someone who had just walked out of a haunted house. He went on for what seemed like hours, recounting every humiliating detail while his father listened intently.

Mason's dad had a unique understanding of his son's troubles. Michael Harvey had been obese as a child. He, too, had been bullied. He still carried the scars of his own childhood shame. Mason could see both the sadness and the anger swelling inside his father. His father was his hero, so Mason thought his dad could fix anything. One reason he'd hesitated to tell him for nearly the entire school year was his concern that his dad might actually storm up to school and hurt someone.

"I was afraid my dad might get arrested," Mason says with a hint of fear and a pinch of male pride.

Mike Harvey promised his son the problem would be dealt with immediately. He and Julie agreed Mike would go to the school the very next day. They'd long suspected something was wrong. Mike knew the signs but had held on to hope that his boy would have a different childhood than he'd experienced.

One of the many benefits of living in a small town like Guthrie is that most people know one another. There is often a common history. Mason's school counselor had been a childhood friend and classmate of his father's. Supportive and kind, the counselor recommended moving Mason to another class. But moving Mason was only a partial solution. The bullies just made better use of the time in the hallway, in the cafeteria, and on the playground.

"If I was walking to class, they'd come up on each side of me and, like, play tennis with me. Push me back and forth," Mason says, describing the humiliation. Mason's parents were soon back at the counselor's office and then the principal's office. Administrators shared his parents' concern. A counselor recommended that Mason try to shield himself from the insults.

"I think it was called the duck method or something like that," Mason recalls. Mason was encouraged to imagine he was a duck with wings and then use his wings to cover his ears and block out the noise whenever he was confronted by one of his bullies.

Mason tried it for about three days. Either his wings were not big enough or the bullies ignored ducks just like they ignored the teachers who told them to leave Mason alone. Frustrated, Mason went back to his old ways; he suffered in silence and soothed his hurt with food while he waited for the end of the year. Third grade was almost over. Fourth grade had to be better.

After a joyous summer of playing with his brothers and cousins, taking long rides in the car with his parents, and visiting a few amusement parks, it was back to school. Maybe the bullies had changed schools? Maybe they'd find someone else to pick on? Next to praying for good grades, Mason just prayed for a peaceful year at school: a bully-free zone. At least there would be more extracurricular activities to choose from.

"There was band, and we had a bigger PE room. Lots of my friends were in my class. That's what helped me. The boys were not in my class, and I didn't see 'em in the hallways much."

But when he did encounter the bullies, they picked up right where they'd left off. With age their insults were becoming more vulgar and profane. Raised never to curse, Mason couldn't even bring himself to repeat the language the bullies used. Instead he just let the words pile up inside him like garbage in a trash can.

Mason began to adjust his school day to avoid the boys. "Usually during recess I'd come inside to study instead of going outside. Because I knew if I'd go outside, they'd probably continue."

But even when the bullying was at its worst, his grades never fell below a B. He also loved sports. If it involved a ball and the outdoors, Mason was all in.

Football was his first love, the Green Bay Packers and
the New England Patriots his favorite pro teams. But
the sun rose and set with the Oklahoma State University Cowboys. In Oklahoma you are either a Sooner
or a Cowboy. Mason bled OSU Cowboy black and
orange. Truth be told, his love for sports ran deeper
than his love for school. Unfortunately his talent did
not match his desires in football or any other sport.

In football Mason was always on the offensive
or defensive line because of his girth. He dreamed of
scoring touchdowns, something linemen rarely do. In
baseball he loved the fast-paced action of the infield
and the pressure of the pitcher's mound. But once again
because of his weight, Mason's coaches always put him
in the outfield.

"I guess they put me out there because I was so
slow," Mason says.

Outfield can be a lonely position, especially in
Little League. The ball rarely came his way, teammates
mostly ignored him, and fans barely noticed him at
games. Baseball started to feel like school, and football was not much better. Morbidly obese, tormented

at school, sidelined in sports, Mason Harvey realized he did not feel good about himself. Adults talked and talked about self-esteem. Mason knew he did not have much of it left.

One of the Harvey brothers' favorite haunts was the local skating rink. Their parents often took them skating as a reward for good behavior or a stellar report card. One night Mason's troubles followed him to the rink. He'd taken a break from skating and laughing with his friends when a couple of boys approached him. He did not know them by name, but they were familiar faces at the rink.

"Hey, fat boy! You're too fat to skate! What are you doing here?"

Even at the skating rink Mason was no longer safe. The guys moved closer. Their eyes were menacing. They began to lean in. But suddenly, without warning, they stopped dead in their tracks. They looked past Mason as if they had seen a ghost. No ghost. It was Mason's older brother, Brennan. Brennan was tall and lean, noticeably muscular for a kid his age.

"I suggest you boys move on. Whatever your problem, you want none of this," Brennan said. His voice had already deepened. He sounded like a man. The bullies backed off like freshly whupped dogs. A surge of energy and joy rushed through Mason's body. Part of him wanted to chase after the bullies, tackle them, and give them a good beating. Instead he turned and hugged his big brother.

"I was just bawling," Mason recalls with a wide grin. His brother responded like a true teenage older sibling: "Dude, no tears on the shirt." The moment was over. Order restored. Mason knew his brother was not much into sentimentality. But he also knew his brother had his back.

"He's always been one to stick up for me. He's always been a friend to me . . . because every time I'm somewhere, he'll stick up for me if something goes wrong. And I love him and cherish him for that."

But his brother couldn't shadow him at school. Mason had to do something for himself.

By age ten going on eleven, Mason says, he became "sick and tired of being sick and tired." Little did he know he was quoting the legendary civil rights activist

Fannie Lou Hamer. Back in 1964 she told the world she was sick and tired of the sins of segregation in the South. She knew pain and humiliation based on race. It was one of the ugliest chapters of American history. Hers was a suffering Mason could never imagine, but on some levels he could relate. He was mistreated, undervalued, and often made to feel invisible because of his weight. And just like Fannie Lou Hamer, Mason decided to do something about his situation.

"I decided to take it upon myself that I was just tired of it all around," Mason says, "so I told my parents about being heavy. I told them I didn't want to be heavy anymore."

It usually takes a spark, a final straw, for someone to make a change. Mason's straw was his inhaler.

His parents had gotten him an inhaler during football season because Mason was so overweight he had a hard time breathing. As much as he needed the device, Mason found it humiliating. While his teammates would run to the sideline to splash their faces with water, sip Gatorade, or strategize for the next series of plays, Mason would be fumbling for his inhaler.

"I just . . . felt it in my body because it got harder for me to breathe, and I had to drink a lot of water and . . . come off the field sometime to get more water and get more air in my lungs. I couldn't ever stay with my team. Whenever we were doing running drills in practice, I'd always be the caboose."

Between the embarrassment of the inhaler and the constant bullying, Mason had had enough by sixth grade. Something had to change.

Like a lot of boys his age, Mason was starting to pay attention to muscle magazines and programs on television about fitness. He even started to see his own body change as he got older and continued to play sports. *What if I start exercising on my own?* he thought. *Maybe I could lose weight.*

At first he wanted to lose weight just so he could lose his inhaler.

But that was enough motivation to start.

The summer between sixth and seventh grade Mason created his own exercise routine. He asked his parents to take him to the local YMCA, where he joined a strength training class and learned to use the equipment. He would run to places to which he used to walk, took swimming lessons, and spent more time on the trampoline in the backyard. He played more and ran harder that summer than he ever had his entire life.

If he lost enough weight and gained enough speed, Mason thought, maybe the coaches would move him from the line to the backfield. If not a running back, then perhaps a fullback. Maybe he might even score a touchdown.

Just the thought of all the possibilities made him smile and run faster. And day by day the pounds seemed to fall off. More than that, though, Mason was feeling better about himself.

It wasn't long before summer was over. When he went back to school, the most amazing thing occurred. Mason got out of his mom's car like he had every day of every school year and made his way to the door. People were staring at him. Even his friends were looking at him differently. Finally one classmate approached him.

"Mason, what happened to you? You've changed," the friend said with sheer amazement in his voice. After a summer of exercising and playing and spending as much time outside as possible, and therefore less time at the dinner table, Mason had lost nearly forty pounds. He was a new person. Or at least he looked like a new person.

"It felt good coming to seventh grade for the first day of school and having all these guys looking at me like I'm a stranger. 'You guys know me. Why are you looking at me like that?'" he says with a smile.

The energy Mason had once devoted to hiding in fear from the school bullies was now channeled into a healthier lifestyle. And this eleven-year-old figured out, on his own, that more change had to come from the inside.

"I decided to invest, I guess, in . . . websites, and I would look at the foods and see what they had in them, how much calories or how bad it would be for me or how good it would be for me. And a lot of it said that if you do eat junk food, just try and watch your portion intake on it. And that's what I was not doing when I was younger."

Over the course of the school year he would lose another forty-five pounds through exercise and diet.

"What probably pushed me was probably my

anger . . . because whenever I get really mad, I feel like I can do more. During football if somebody were to knock me down . . . or put me on the ground, I feel like I have to come back and get them. So it probably would have been my anger that told me to not give up, because I felt like I could overcome the bullies and not be their victim anymore."

Mason Harvey lost eighty-five pounds in ten months through his own sweat and some tears. He encouraged his parents to improve their eating habits and got his dad to join him at the gym. He now snacks on carrot sticks instead of chips, and today the family spends more time planning their meals to include healthy choices.

"A lot of people ask me how I look back at what I used to eat and how I'm not getting so tempted to eat it again. And it's actually pretty hard. You've just got to have a determination to not do it. And if you still eat junk food, just don't eat a lot of it like I used to. I'll still have a hamburger once in a while, but it won't be an all-day, every-day meal for me. Most of the time I'm trying to eat healthy."

By age twelve Mason Harvey was taking control

44

of his life. No more bullies. No more fears. Some had moved away, but the others chose to stay clear of the new Mason. "I felt like the boys had complete control over me and I couldn't do anything about it. But I showed them wrong."

To meet Mason today is to meet the same sweet-tempered guy he always was. He's wiser, leaner, and more thoughtful, perhaps, but not at all regretful about what he endured. "Losing weight didn't change me," Mason says. It just changed how the world saw him, even on the baseball field, where he finally moved from the outfield to the infield the next season. "I was a pitcher. I played first base, and sometimes they played me on third."

Soon Mason went from Little Leaguer to motivational speaker. He created a website called Strive for 85, where he encouraged other people, especially young people, to embrace healthy eating. He's appeared in newspapers and magazines and on national television spreading his gospel about living a healthy lifestyle. His efforts and reputation even got the attention of the White House and First Lady Michelle Obama! In 2012 she invited him to the annual White House Easter Egg Roll. "She gave me a hug. I felt like a million bucks."

Just as Mason was getting accustomed to his new-found celebrity, he was diagnosed with type 1 diabetes. But like bullying and obesity, it hasn't kept him down.

"My struggle with my weight taught me the power of focus and hard work. I'll manage. No, I'll excel. I have a great future."

Where do you go, where do you hide, when the world hurts too much? For Mason the answer is: "My family. My parents and brothers have always loved me no matter what. They don't judge. They don't hurt me. That's not to say they don't get angry with me every now and then. But I always can count on them."

PAPPY

"I would rather die free than live as a slave."

I t sounded like just another severe rainstorm in Bukavu, the capital of Sud-Kivu, in Zaire (now called the Democratic Republic of the Congo). The pounding rat-a-tat on the metal roofs in the neighborhood, followed by the crackling sound of thunder and the blinding flash of lightning, was familiar to the students who lived in the rain forest in central Africa. What seemed curious to twelve-year-old Pappy and his classmates was why their teachers were overly animated, running and yelling at students to stand in doorways and lie on the ground. Teachers raising their voices at students was nothing new, but this seemed extreme. Pappy and his friends had been raised to respect authority, so all they could do was comply and wonder aloud why all the commotion.

With little warning the administration abruptly dismissed class for the day. Students at the Agape's secondary school were ordered to get home as quickly as possible. Once outside, Pappy and his friends understood the urgency. What they had thought was crackling thunder was actually sporadic gunfire and bombs striking their village. The flashes of light were the buildings and homes in this once peaceful and stable community being ripped apart by explosions. The year was 1996, and twelve-year-old Boyinkebe Orion "Pappy" Rwizibuka's life was about to change forever.

For all of his dozen years Pappy had proudly carried the moniker of a firstborn son. Part of his name, Boyinkebe, means "to sit," and by African tradition the firstborn male should one day sit in the place of his father. Pappy was the oldest son, with lots of sisters and younger brothers. His mother had been pregnant nearly every year, and now there were children ranging in age from preteens to toddlers. Ten in all.

Louis Rwizibuka, Pappy's father, had a prominent government job in his village. He was the equivalent of a US tax collector. Having no computer, he kept fastidious handwritten records of everyone who lived in the town, where they worked, and how much they owed. With his income, he could afford to provide his family with a large six-bedroom brick house on the outskirts of town. Pappy admired and respected his father and hoped to take his place at the head of a large family one day. It was a good life.

Each day Pappy walked to school in his crisp white uniform shirt and blue pants. The schoolboys favored American-style sneakers. He wore white Adidases with black stripes. He could have afforded transportation to school, but Pappy preferred to walk, taking his time in the often humid and oppressive heat. He had always enjoyed the extra time with classmates. In forty-five minutes he would arrive at his school or back home.

But on this day Pappy was running for his life. "We were running home when one of my classmates fell down," Pappy recalls. More so out of curiosity than concern, Pappy and a few of his classmates ran back to their fallen comrade. Had he stumbled, or was he so slow he could not keep up?

It was a time of great turmoil in Zaire, a country bigger than Alaska, California, and Montana put together. The president of Zaire, a man named Mobutu Sese Seko, was not liked by many of the neighboring countries. While he strongly advanced Zaire's national pride, he was seen as ego-driven and obsessed with wealth and power. During his thirty-one-year reign, there had been several attempts to remove Mobutu from the presidency. Seven other African nations were now lining up to fight against him. And much of the opposition was growing in the southeastern part of Zaire, where Pappy lived.

Pappy's village of Bukavu was on the border with Rwanda, and there had been a civil war for many years in the neighboring country. At one time fighting there between the Hutu and Tutsi tribes had led to a genocide of eight hundred thousand people in just ninety days. Over the years Hutu forces escaping from Rwanda had set up camps in areas near where Pappy lived. They would then sneak back across the border to attack the Tutsi in Rwanda. Now Rwanda was fully engaged in bringing the battle to Zairean soil, and this would spark the latest attempt to overthrow the Mobutu. As the fighting raged, the bloodshed was spilling into Pappy's neighborhood.

And now Pappy could see it firsthand. Blood was soaking through his classmate's shirt. His friend was dead. Shot in the back. Pappy and his friends screamed and cried. They were frozen with fear but couldn't be for long. The searing heat of chaos and killing thawed their shock quickly. Pappy needed to run to the one place that had always been safe . . . home.

"When I got home, my parents weren't there. We wouldn't see them for days," says Pappy. As someone who was widely known to have worked for Zaire's embattled President Mobutu, Pappy's father was a target of the antigovernment fighters. Once the war arrived in Bukavu, Louis Rwizibuka had to leave home for long periods of time or stay with relatives to protect himself. Sometimes he was able to take his wife or a few of his younger children. But Pappy would often have to sleep in the woods at night or stay in the homes of strangers. Suddenly, carefree Pappy was learning the meaning of fear. Wanting to appear strong for his relatives, and with his father's encouragement, he said to himself and anyone who'd listen that he was convinced the chaos would end as quickly as it had started.

The uprising was swift, and within months Mobutu's government had fallen. The family thought it was finally safe to return home for good.

They were wrong. The cycle of war was just beginning, and before long more fighting broke out. There was already opposition to the replacement government, and rebel groups were springing up. The family never felt safe, and Pappy's parents were once again forced to flee. Pappy was left in charge of the house and his siblings. They were left to fend for themselves and were running out of food. With the sounds of war drawing closer to their doorstep night after night, the task was daunting. Pappy had never cared much for chores. Though his parents always insisted cleanliness was next to godliness, he had never bought into the concept. But now he was in charge of making sure the chores were done and everyone was fed. Not long after, his authority was challenged from the outside.

The rebels who had months earlier turned a school playground into a killing field were now going from neighborhood to neighborhood, house to house, ransacking homes, stealing property, and raping the women and girls.

"They took my sister, and I went after them. I had to negotiate her release." Sadness seeps into Pappy's voice as he recalls the episode. He managed to track the location where his younger sister was being held. The rebels had kept her in a building crowded with men for at least five days. Pappy could hear her screams. He knew what was happening. The sounds of her pain hit him like blows to the head. His little sister was eight years old.

Everything changed that day.

Eventually the rebels let her go. But the same horror

was later repeated on another of Pappy's sisters. A five-year-old sister. Her attackers carried the AIDS virus, which the little girl contracted. She died years later.

"I think of her often and what her life could have been. In time I learned to believe [that] because she died and how she died, I had to live. And someday live well. For me 'someday' was as much a place as it was a point in time."

Each time Pappy and his family endured one horror, their reward was a new one. And a growing number of the most violent perpetrators were Pappy's age. Kids as young as nine, ten, eleven, and twelve years old turned into soldiers. The label "child soldier" sounds almost cartoonish, but there was nothing remotely comical about the brutality they were capable of and what all of them endured. Most of them had been beaten, drugged, and indoctrinated with hate. Kids not yet drafted endured equal depravity.

The rebels then captured one of Pappy's uncles, a once-powerful man in local government. Before the rebels killed him, they gathered up Pappy and other children in the family to watch as their uncle was tortured. One day his lower lip was cut off, grilled, and fed back to him. Another day his hands were cut off. The next day it was his forearms. This went on until the life was literally cut out of the man.

The children were forced to watch at gunpoint, standing still, not allowed to scream or cry or make a single sound.

"I can't explain it, but I literally lost the ability to cry," Pappy says. "It takes time to cry. I needed every moment to stay alive," he adds. Not yet a man, Pappy was no longer a boy. He was trapped somewhere in the middle. A limbo. He was alive, but his soul was dying.

Pappy's father—who got word to his family as often as he could while in hiding—eventually made his way back home. He somehow convinced his captors he was not a flight risk and would prove more valuable as a village mediator while back at home with his family. Pappy suspects someone in the family may have paid a bribe. Whatever allowed him to return to his family, Pappy's father could see the changes in his son and in his country. A devout Roman Catholic, with a small farm and a respected job, Louis had

had honorable dreams for all of his children. Dreams that now seemed impossible. Much of the Congo had fallen into chaos. Rival rebel factions were killing one another and the innocent. Friends and relatives were approaching him to determine the availability of his sons, interested in recruiting them to become child soldiers. Now thirteen, Pappy was the ripe age, smart and surprisingly strong for a boy his size. At five feet two inches tall, he had the build of a fire hydrant atop Adidas sneakers. One uncle insisted Pappy should join his militia, known as a Mai-Mai. It was better he fight with family than fight against them, the uncle insisted. But Pappy's father had another idea. He was secretly planning to send his son away from the fighting. If Pappy could escape the Congo and survive, he could find a noble family to work for.

"My father would rather I be a slave than a child soldier," Pappy says.

Once his decision was made, Louis Rwizibuka acted quickly. "We had just finished eating, and my dad just came to me and said, 'I love you, but I have to send you away because I don't want you to join any of these movements.' I thought it was a joke. But he was quite serious. 'I have arranged everything, and this day at four o'clock in the morning we will leave and we will show you the way to go.'"

His father had sewn two hundred dollars into a secret compartment in Pappy's pants. He had arranged with two other families to send their boys as well. Each carried equally large sums of money. That very night they hugged their parents and Pappy cried. "Why would you want to let me go?" he asked his father. His father said, "I don't know how you're going to end up living, but I know that God will protect you. And whatever you end up doing, never forget your family. And never forget your people."

Then, stealing away in the dark so no one would see them, the three boys took a bus from their village to the border and crossed into Rwanda. As the old and creaky bus snaked down the dusty road belching smoke, they looked back at their parents. They knew the chances of seeing them again were faint. All they could see ahead was uncertainty.

Three boys on their own, less than a thousand

dollars between them. They carried backpacks with a few clothes and a little food, and the hopes, fears, and prayers of their families.

And so began the dangerous adventure of thirteen-year-old Pappy Rwizibuka. A two-and-a-half-year journey that would sound like the exploits of a young Indiana Jones. He was headed into uncertain and often unfriendly territory. The fifty-four nations of Africa are populated by thousands of tribal groups speaking nearly two thousand different languages. Many of the tribes had long been enemies. Pappy had no particular destination and no adult to guide him, and would undoubtedly lack the language skills to seek help along the way. He was also joining thousands of other Congolese refugees who were fleeing the violence in their homeland. They would flood the countries nearby as most unwelcome guests, all seeking the same necessities as Pappy—safety and freedom.

Since Pappy and his friends were members of the Hutu tribe and Congolese refugees, escaping into Tutsi-led Rwanda was dangerous, but heading east was the quickest and closest path away from the Congo. If they were captured, their families hoped they would be put in prison or put to work. Both were better options than the brutality of life as a child soldier.

"My dad thought of that. I think it was because of his strong church. He is a man of faith, and as a child, he learned much about that. What does God want for us? Does he want us to kill people? Does he want us to rape people? Nor does he want us to be horrible people."

So the three traveled by night and rested in the daytime. It was safer to navigate after dark, when the Rwandan soldiers were asleep and the temperature was cooler. Without a compass or maps, they followed the roads. "Often we just followed the moon." Constantly running from skirmishes and gunfire, they attempted to return to the Congo within weeks but were driven back by more rebel fighting. Some friendly villagers suggested that they head into the country of Burundi and seek help from the Congolese embassy. When they arrived in the capital city of Bujumbura, it had been weeks since they had eaten any real food. They rarely dared to enter a village in daylight, let alone a market. So having exhausted their food supplies, they were surviving on leaves and plants and the occasional banana. When they had no water to drink, they drank their own urine. Hungry, dirty, and smelling like thirteen-year-olds who had not bathed in weeks, they virtually collapsed at the embassy door. They might have been the youngest trio, but they were not the only people looking for help. The place was crowded with refugees.

Pappy and his friends were like specks of sand on an ocean floor of misery. The adults around them could make a better case for their needs, and the children younger than Pappy's group must have looked more desperate than the adolescent boys. Thus the embassy was little help; however, they were given travel documents and were advised to make their way to Zambia. The fastest and presumably safest route was by ferryboat on Lake Tanganyika, one of the longest and deepest lakes in the world. It runs about 420 miles and touches four different countries. The length of the lake was daunting, but it was the depth that scared the boys most. None of them could swim.

"So when we got to the ferry, we negotiated with the captain. He was Congolese and he understood the situation in [the] Congo. So he accepted to take us to Zambia. Stop in Tanzania. But he had to hide us in the engine room of the ferry. So we had to spend about three days in this engine room. It was very hot . . . [so after] about a day and a half we decided to come out because it was so hot. But when we came out, there were soldiers on board."

The rebel soldiers were also headed to Zambia and were surprised and angry about the presence of these Congolese boys. At his age, Pappy could very well have been an enemy soldier. It was yet another moment when he feared he was about to die.

"In [the] Congo I knew that one day already I was going to be killed. When I saw my friend [running from school], actually, I thought I was going to die. And when I was in Rwanda, I thought that we were going to be captured and we were going to be killed. Because we were quite scared of the Rwandese, and on the ferry to Zambia I was scared. I thought this was the end of my life."

But the boat captain stepped in and risked his own life to save theirs.

"These soldiers started questioning us . . . what we were doing there, and they wanted to throw us into the lake. But the captain pleaded. Was on his knees, crying, 'These kids are related to me. You cannot throw them out of the boat.' And luckily they accepted to let us go."

So the three-day journey down Lake Tanganyika was tense, but peaceful thanks to the brave intervention of the ferry captain. It was a kindness they were to see very little of during the rest of their journey. "In Zambia we talked to each other and decided to change some money from the money our parents had given us. We wanted to change to kwacha [the currency in Zambia]. One of my friends had four hundred dollars, and another had two hundred dollars. In Zambia we exchanged all of my friend's two hundred dollars because we didn't know the value of the exchange. They gave us the value of twenty dollars."

The boys were learning they could trust no one but themselves. "We didn't realize we were being robbed, people just kept asking for our money."

A kind greeting or warm smile from a stranger was often just a trap. Occasionally they took a bus or negotiated for a high-priced ride in a truck or car. And quickly their parents' money was disappearing. At one river crossing they were forced to give up not only money, but also a watch, a bracelet, and a school backpack in exchange for safe passage.

"We don't want you here" was the one consistent message that Pappy and his friends received at every stop.

In the Zambian city of Mpulungu, just across the border from Tanzania, they were advised that the capital, Lusaka, might be the best place for them. It was more than six hundred miles away, a long and tiring distance for three hungry, exhausted, and homesick teenagers. But they pushed on, spending endless hours hiding inside boxes on transport trucks taking the same route. Pappy remembers that it took "a long time" to get to Lusaka, probably months. It was another destination that they hoped would be the end of their road, where they could find work, perhaps a home, and where they could wait for the war in the Congo to end so they could return to their families. At each stop along their journey they were convinced safety and a better life were just over the next rise. They soon realized they were fooling themselves. Every new village, almost every place they paused to rest, had its own challenges. Different faces. Familiar hardships.

"In Lusaka we stayed there for two months or so, and again we couldn't survive there. People were harassing us. They were beating us up. We would exchange our money and they would take everything, and so we . . . decided to keep going."

They had crossed thirteen hundred miles, most of it on foot. More than a year had now passed, and they had not found a safe home. But they were still alive and they considered that a blessing. "Also the fact that my parents might still be alive and that I would be able to see them one day. That's another thing that kept me going. You cannot die, because your parents will grow old and not see you growing old."

Some of the land they had traversed was the most spectacular in all of Africa, but they'd hardly had the time or inclination to appreciate it. Forced to leave

Zambia, they crossed the Zambezi River into Zimbabwe near Victoria Falls. For tourists from around the world, including Americans, it is a place of rare beauty. One of the most wondrous sites in all the world. Tourists pay thousands of dollars to see Victoria Falls, go on safari to spot rare and dangerous animals, and enjoy the exotic vistas. The boys did it for free. They were not tourists. Surrounded by wild animals, they were suddenly part of the food chain.

The message in Zimbabwe was much the same as in other countries: "Go someplace else." This time they were told that South Africa was welcoming Congolese refugees and they would find a better life there. But border guards would not allow them to enter South Africa without travel documents and visas, which Pappy and his friends could not acquire. The only alternative was to sneak in across a crocodile-infested river. Many others had died trying to make this crossing. The boys' options seemed to have finally run out. And with that news a kind of despair began to fill Pappy. After nearly two years of traveling he thought about giving up.

"Life became very meaningless. You think about

[how you believed that if] you get to this particular town, you will be much better. You will be protected and you will have a good life. [It] is not so. So at that particular time you want to take your own life, and that's what I wanted to do. If you get to that point where you want to take your own life, I don't think you can go any lower."

Hopelessness brings desperation, and Pappy had finally reached his lowest point. "At that time desperation has led us to believe in the powers of the devil. Anything that can take us from a place to another. We will believe in that. It doesn't matter what they do."

It was always in these moments, the depths of despair, that he could hear his father's voice and his words of insistence: "Pray, boy! Always pray." For much of his childhood, religion had been mostly a ritual for Pappy, something his family had engaged in for generations. Now his faith had meaning. Many nights he would go to bed hungry, but prayer and the words in the Bible verses he'd memorized fed his soul. He felt both an emotional and a spiritual lift, knowing the words he uttered in the evenings were similar to the words he'd heard his father and other family members use. Faith, like his daily circumstances, was hard to explain. One zapped his strength. The other gave him the will to try again the next day. A mix of desperation and faith allowed Pappy to see opportunity. He'd already seen the worst of people and the good. He chose to believe better days were ahead. How soon he didn't know. Still, staying hopeful, like staying alive, was almost a daily challenge.

Pappy and his friends eventually hired a local guide who could take them by boat across the river, but the guide advised the trio to meet a local witch doctor. Rumor had it he was skilled at getting refugees safely across the Limpopo River into South Africa. Pappy was hesitant. He was a Christian. What would his father, a devout Catholic, think of his son seeking the advice of a witch doctor? Pappy had to get over his hesitation. To this point, the journey had taught him to believe whatever he needed to believe in order to survive. As payment, the witch doctor made them give up all of their belongings. For two nights he treated them with his spells of protection. Then he walked the boys to the edge of the river and Pappy saw him sprinkle something in the water. He told them to enter the water and that they would be safe. And the crocodiles moved away, like when Moses parted the Red Sea in the Bible.

"And you could see crocodiles going that side . . . and crocodiles going that side wherever we were to cross. I don't know which kind of power allowed him to do that kind of thing that he did there. And I don't know who really protected us at that particular moment. [But we] could pass in the middle. And literally see the crocodiles this side and that side. It was amazing . . . crazy."

The boys crossed the river unharmed. They arrived in a national park. They walked for many days, looking for someone who might take them to a refugee camp.

They finally stumbled upon a military encampment, where the soldiers fed them milk and porridge. The next day the soldiers turned the teenagers over to the local police, who put them on a train to Johannesburg. From Johannesburg they made their way to Cape Town, and there, at the tip of the African continent, there was seemingly no place left for them to go.

The Red Cross took them in for a few months, but

soon they were on their own. Bed space was limited, and they eventually grew restless. "There had to be more to life than this refugee camp." Pappy would often tell this to himself and any of his friends who'd listen.

For a time they slept under a bridge and ate from garbage cans. They found odd jobs selling fruits and vegetables on the street and later washing car windshields at red lights. From middle-class schoolboy to squeegee boy in two years. Prospects for a bright future were beyond dim; at the time they seemed pitch black.

So Pappy thought he had gotten the break of a lifetime when he met a Nigerian businessman who offered him work. It turned out he was a drug dealer and child molester. He put Pappy to work as a drug mule. Pappy had traveled 2,292 miles to escape the violence of war in his hometown of Bukavu, and now he was facing a new kind of brutality.

"At some point I decided that I just need to die. I can't take it anymore. I didn't know if my parents [were] alive, what was happening. One day I went to the train station and jumped in front of a moving train, but I didn't die. I just threw myself and I was still okay."

Pappy fell short of the train and onto his face. The cool breeze of the passing railcars actually felt refreshing. The taste of dust in his mouth reminded him he was both alive and hungry. For a moment he imagined the mix of saliva and dirt was delicious-tasting peanut butter. The pain of his scraped elbows and knees shook him back to reality. He was still alive and life was still very hard.

Tired and desperate, he decided to rob his employer and move to the next town. But the drug dealer caught him and put a gun to his head. As the Nigerian began to pull the trigger, his wife pleaded for Pappy's life. The drug dealer let him live. At that moment Pappy realized he had a choice, either to keep dying or to start living. One of his friends from home had already become addicted to drugs and was lost to the streets. Pappy never saw him again.

With the promise of work in a small shop, Pappy found a way to move to a small town called Worcester. Hardship had taught Pappy the value of being valuable. Name an odd job, he could do it: minor repairs, manual labor, street vending. Though small in stature, he'd learned to make a big impression on people with either his work effort or his wit. People liked having him around. NGOs (nongovernmental organizations) were beginning to sprout up like dandelions. Some groups offered food, others offered work, and more and more were providing an opportunity at an education. Pappy knew a shot at an education would be a game changer. His back and his bravado could take him but so far. So Pappy made himself valuable to one of the NGOs that advocated educating refugee children. People took notice of his drive and desire to learn. Eventually he was invited to enroll for free in a Christian school. He attributed his good fortune to pure luck and perseverance. He'd learned an important lesson he would cling to for his lifetime: A big part of success is just persevering. Struggle. Fall. Fear. Frustration. Sleep. Try again the next day. He knew the discovery wasn't groundbreaking or profound, but it had kept him alive.

At school he met boys and girls his age who seemed like they were from a different planet. Since the day he left his family in the Congo, he'd spent almost every waking hour consumed by one thing: finding food.

Now he was in a place where children talked about their dreams and education and careers. Pappy knew he was not in heaven, but he thought he was close. By chance, an American pastor from North Carolina named William Bryant visited the school one day along with his family, and Pappy gave them a tour. Reverend Bryant was immediately drawn to Pappy's life story. While he was in South Africa, he ministered to Pappy, offered him financial support, and kept his word to stay in touch when he returned to the United States.

"And that's when life began to get better for me, at the age of seventeen."

A person can drive from Bukavu to Cape Town in five days. Or make it by plane in a few hours. Pappy made it on foot, ferryboat, buses, the backs of trucks, and cargo trains in two and a half years. He lived a lifetime in thirty months, relying on his own wits and the kindness of strangers.

It was not until 2007 that Pappy finally returned to the Democratic Republic of the Congo. Here is how he describes his homecoming:

"It was with a mixture of pain and joy as I crossed

back into my country, the place of my birth. My family had been on the move almost the entire time I had been away; it had been too dangerous for them to stay in one place. I managed to track them down and was overwhelmed with emotion when, at last, we were reunited. I wanted to hold them and never let them go.

"I stayed with them a week, and though my heart was glad to see them, I could see the years had brought much pain to their lives. My father and mother were thin and looked old. They were not the same people I had left behind. I knew they had seen much suffering.

"The day I left my beloved country, I looked at every member of my family and the entire population in my beautiful village and prayed that the suffering and pain I saw would one day be replaced with hope and that peace would once again be restored."

Today Pappy lives in Germany, where he works for a relief agency called Youth With A Mission. His vision is to return to the Congo someday to open a school and educate the children who have been affected by war, specifically the child soldiers. "I lost much of my childhood, and that I will always regret. But I learned things about myself, the spirit within me. Strife has taught me there is no time to waste. No time for bitterness. No time for self-pity. I was allowed to live for a reason. I believe that reason is to serve. Save someone else. There is a Pappy out there waiting for me. Waiting to hear my whisper: 'Hold on. You can make it.'"

Where do you go, where do you hide, when the world hurts too much? For Pappy the answer is: "The church. I was raised in a Christian household. During the worst of the fighting the one place people still felt safe was inside the walls of the church. As I made my way to South Africa, I discovered that the church lived in me. My faith helped carry me to safety."

MICHAELA

"I am a fighter."

To see Michaela Sanderson walk across her college campus is to see a young woman with the poise of a second-year law student, the spirit of a varsity cheerleader, and the looks of the pretty girl next door. Conventional wisdom says that the world and its opportunities are wide open for girls like Michaela: blond, smart, athletic, ambitious, and confident.

On the August day in 2012 when she arrived as a freshman at the University of Alabama, eighteen-year-old Michaela was giddy with excitement about meeting her new roommates and seeing her dorm room for the first time.

"I love meeting new people and getting to know what they like and stuff. It sounds really exciting to me."

The weekend before classes started, Michaela and her three roommates set up their dorm rooms, put away all their clothes, hung pictures on the wall, and stocked up on groceries. A similar scene was being repeated all across the Tuscaloosa campus.

Michaela could have had her pick of colleges. She finished with a perfect 4.0 in high school and was ranked sixth in her class. But she did not want to travel too far from her hometown, so she chose the Tuscaloosa campus of the University of Alabama, where she could one day get a PhD in her chosen field of social work. Someday she wants to help kids like herself, whom she describes this way:

"A kid from a broken home who just feels alone."

Alone.

On a campus of thirty thousand students, with

roommates close by, and with an outgoing personality that easily attracted new friends, Michaela still felt alone. Because no one knew who she really was and what she had been through.

"I feel like I've lost everyone. I've lost my parents. I've lost my siblings. I'm not really in contact with them besides my twin. Everybody that you would think would be there in the end isn't now."

Most of UA's students come from somewhere in the state. Michaela traveled only sixty-seven miles from the town of Gardendale, Alabama, to Tuscaloosa, but in practical terms it might as well have been the distance between Gardendale and Mars. Michaela was a long, long way from where she'd started.

"We grew up really poor. We lived in the projects, and our houses were always molded, and one of our houses was roach infested. We didn't have money for food. We got food from food banks and we had food stamps."

Michaela was born in Birmingham. Her mom, Olivia, was twenty-nine years old when she gave birth to twin girls, Michaela and her sister, Danielle. Her dad,

Michael, was thirty-seven. Her parents had three older children from previous marriages and two together, so the twins were the youngest of seven. Michaela and her twin were closest to their older brother Jesse and an older sister, Mary Elizabeth, whom they called Boo Boo. Those four all had the same mom and dad.

For as long as Michaela could remember, there were drugs around the house.

Michaela remembers her mom using marijuana, prescription pills, uppers, downers. Drug addiction was rampant in her family tree, with close relatives and siblings all struggling with addiction at one point or another. Boo Boo assumed the caretaking role in the family.

"She was like our mom figure 'cause she was eight years older than me and my twin sister. 'Cause my mom was always passed out on the couch. So my sister did what she could when Mommy was sick."

And when her mom was not passed out, she was often fighting with Michaela's father. "They fought a lot when I was little, like fistfights and things of that nature. So my mom ran from my dad a lot. That's why we moved so much. We moved from school to school."

By the time she entered high school, Michaela had been to thirteen different schools. The school year would always either start or finish the same way: her mother back with her father, and Michaela knowing there was little value in making new friends.

At one point the four youngest kids moved in with their father. Michaela was in first grade. It was the closest thing to "family" that she had ever experienced. But Boo Boo was sick. Dying, in fact. She had only one lung, and it was full of tumors. Eventually her esophagus collapsed, and she could barely eat for two and a half years. So it was an additional burden for her to try to care for her younger sisters.

"To this day I'm not certain of her exact cause of death. Like cancer, it was a disease that ate away at her body. She was sixteen when she died." Few times in life had Michaela felt more alone. Her family may have been dysfunctional, but it was her family. And it was steadily falling apart.

It was around that time that the family came to the attention of Alabama's Department of Human

Resources. The children's frequent school changes had not gone unnoticed. Michaela was now eight. She and her twin sister were taken away and put in a group home for a few nights, then they moved in with one of their father's relatives. They lived there for a year.

Eventually the girls were allowed to move back in with their mother. They loved her and missed her, despite Olivia's mood swings and erratic behavior.

"I don't want to make her sound like a bad person, because she really was like the most loving person ever and she loved everyone." By this stage of life Michaela had learned to compartmentalize how she felt about herself and those she loved. She was not in denial about her mother, but she could separate the good from the bad. Call it foolish, but it allowed her to get up every day.

If anything mattered more to Michaela than her own well-being, it was her twin, Danielle. Both sisters had their growth spurt early and were tall and skinny by fourth grade. Danielle kept growing, and now she is four inches taller than her sister. But back then they could share clothes, wearing the same pants over and over each week, while swapping their T-shirts back and forth. With Boo Boo gone, Michaela had assumed the more adult role. She would set the alarm to get the girls up for school in the morning. And by fifth grade she was doing the laundry and cooking as well.

Not only did her mother have a substance abuse problem, she was also bipolar. The drugs and that disorder made for a dangerous mix. Michaela could see her mother drifting deeper into a hole she might not be able to escape from someday. Her mom constantly threatened suicide, often while fighting with Michaela's dad.

"I remember being at my dad's house in the kitchen and her threatening. She had a knife in her hand and was threatening, just telling me to get out of the room. I was always in the middle of their arguments, trying to break them up. And I wasn't about to leave the room. I was pretty smart. 'Cause I knew she wouldn't do it in front of me."

On several occasions Olivia threatened to stab herself. She had a scar the length of her arm, which she claimed was a scratch. But Michaela's father later admitted that it was a knife wound. She also tried to overdose on pills. Michaela's mother was sick and desperate.

"One time . . . she threatened to run out on the road and get hit by a car." Michaela and the rest of her family always thought Olivia was bluffing in a bid to get attention. At least, Michaela hoped so. To think otherwise was debilitating. "I had to grow up really fast."

Michaela's biggest "growth spurt" came early one morning when she was eleven years old. "We were living with Mom in a trailer home. She had the one bedroom. My sister and I shared a bed in the living room. It was small, but it was ours. Mom seemed in a good place." But one thing was always consistent about Olivia: Good periods were quickly followed by bad. This particular morning was the worst.

"I don't remember the sun being up yet. Momma leaned over me and whispered, 'Where'd you hide the gun?' She said it as if she were whispering me a song. I pretended to be asleep. So she kept asking, and each time I could hear the urgency in her voice. 'Momma, I'm asleep, leave me alone!' is all I kept saying. Eventually she stopped and went back to bed. Relieved, I drifted back to sleep. I can't say how much time had passed, but it wasn't long before she was back. This time more desperate. Shaking me slightly, 'Honey, where is the gun?' Momma and I had agreed weeks earlier it was best if I hid the gun. She'd seemed really depressed for several days. And her depression meant mood swings, grumpier than normal, long spells of dead silence."

Michaela hoped this was just another of those mood swings, so she told her mom where the gun was hidden and fell back to sleep. Circumstance had made Michaela a light sleeper, so in the quiet hours of that early morning she heard a frightening sound. "I heard the gun cock. I knew that was trouble, so I jumped up and ran into Momma's bedroom. She looked at me and put the black-colored pistol to her head. All I could get out was, 'Momma, please!' She then put the gun to her heart and then her stomach. Whether accidentally or intentionally, my mother shot herself in the stomach.

"My immediate instinct was to run and get help.

So dressed in the T-shirt and shorts I slept in, I turned around and ran outside to the volunteer fire department across the street. One of the firemen watched as I ran towards him. He had a welcoming look. I simply said, 'My momma did something stupid!'

"Not long thereafter paramedics, firemen, and police officers were crowded in our small trailer. At the hospital my mother told authorities she shot herself while cleaning her gun. I doubt if anyone believed her."

In the midst of it all, Michaela felt a painful surge of guilt. She'd "let" her mother shoot herself, and she'd run out of the trailer without attending to her sister. The two sisters held each other as the adults moved around them to treat their mother and as their world spiraled further out of control.

"Mom would recover from her injuries, but our lives were changed forever."

One change for Michaela was significant: She had never been a so-called crybaby, but she would make her feelings known. Now she felt she had to take more responsibility for herself and her twin, so Michaela made a choice. "If I needed to cry, I'd go someplace and hide." So she began crawling under her bed or into a dark closet when she felt overwhelmed by the world. "After a good cry I'd feel better. Then I'd get myself together and move on."

Oftentimes for the next several years that routine would be a daily occurrence.

After her mother's failed suicide attempt Michaela and her sister never lived with their mom again. They moved from couch to couch, relative's house to relative's house, for a time. After a few months Child Protective Services took them into custody. For the next two years or so the Sanderson sisters lived with six other girls at the Alabama Baptist Children's Home. "It was one of the best things to ever happen to me in my entire life," Michaela now says. "The house parents who ran the home were a godsend. So kind and loving. They treated us like we were their children. For the first time in as long as I could remember, I felt safe and cared for."

But it seemed like nothing in Michaela's life lasted long. "By the time I was thirteen, we went to live with my mom's cousins Stacy and Johnny. They're good people." A few months after Michaela moved in, her mother died in her sleep. "She had a seizure." Along with all her other health issues, Michaela's mother had also been diagnosed with epilepsy. She hadn't taken her medication for a few days. "I pray she is finally at peace," Michaela says.

Instead of breaking Michaela, the loss of her mother pushed her forward. She was about to enter high school, and she decided to pour herself into her studies and saving money.

"By now I knew I could only control in life what I could control. I might succeed or fail, but with the good Lord and hard work I knew I'd have a chance." Michaela's love for her parents ran deep, but she made the choice that they were part of her, but not all of her. Her parents were her parents. Those were facts. That did not mean their mistakes had to be part of her future. That was her truth. "Facts don't change, but each of us [has] some control over our truths."

Michaela's parents had their good qualities, so she chose to focus on those. Good people came into her life. She might not have had traditional role models, but she had evidence of where good choices could lead and where bad choices could lead. She chose the good path. One of the harder challenges now was not looking back.

Freshman year in high school Michaela made the girls' basketball team, became class president, joined the choir, and took Advanced Placement classes, all while waitressing at a barbecue joint thirty-six hours per week. Over the next three years she'd add more activities, a few more work hours here and there.

By senior year she was a member of the National Honor Society and class treasurer, graduating sixth in her class. "I'm awfully proud of what I accomplished in high school. Didn't many people think I could do it, and there weren't a long line of folks cheering when I got to the finish line. But doing well in high school was just one of many goals I had for my life."

Scholarship offers and college admissions letters filled her mailbox. The college choice had been made early on—"Roll Tide!" The scholarship offers were a different matter. "The most significant was the Horatio Alger Association scholarship. I got to fly on a plane, for the first time, to Washington, DC. Me and about two hundred other scholarship winners from around the country. All kids with stories similar to mine. For the first time in my life I didn't feel alone. There were plenty of kids who had it worse than me, but they managed to push forward. The association members treated us like royalty. Special dinners, classes on etiquette. One of the association members is Supreme Court justice Clarence Thomas. Like the other adults, he was so nice and supportive. We got to go to his office. I met a Supreme Court justice! How cool is that? I've had friends who've been to Disney World and fancy places like that. Going to our nation's capital my senior year in high school to accept my scholarship was my Disney World."

What's the old saying about making chicken salad out of chicken waste? Michaela had figured out the recipe. She took that, her relentless and forever hopeful spirit, the savings she'd earned at Full Moon Bar-B-Que, and the used car she bought on her own, and drove to Tuscaloosa and the University of Alabama.

As you might imagine, college had its ups and

downs, but Michaela got through it the way she had every obstacle in her life: with a relentless work ethic and a willingness to endure. She would still look for a dark place to cry. But each year in college she found herself crying a little less. The stumbling blocks of life started looking more like stepping-stones. Away from her family, she balanced loneliness with the liberating feeling of having to be responsible for only herself. She'd hoped her twin sister would embrace higher education the way she had. But she respected Danielle's choice to focus on work and starting her own family.

Michaela dreams of having her own family someday too. She has other dreams to fulfill first. And she's in a hurry. She graduated from the University of Alabama in three years, in May 2015. Her final GPA was 3.96. "I was bummed I didn't do better. My boyfriend reminds me I did work two jobs during most of college." Now that she has her degree in social work, it's on to graduate school, with dreams of earning her PhD. She is the first member of her family to graduate from college. "I know where I come from, I know the cycles of substance abuse that exist in my family history. But more than that, I know a God who is able. Look at me. He helped me."

But clearly Michaela helped herself.

Michaela Sanderson is well on her way. But before she finished college, life tossed another obstacle in her way. "I've been diagnosed with multiple sclerosis, a neurological disease. There is no known cure. But don't anyone feel sorry for me. They say God never gives you more than you can bear. I'm glad he trusts me. I certainly trust him. In fact, I see my condition as more of a blessing than a burden. As a social worker, I hope to work with people who have debilitating diseases. Tomorrow isn't promised to any of us. I didn't let hardship overwhelm me, why would I let a disease? I'm a fighter."

Where do you go, where do you hide, when the world hurts too much? For Michaela the answer is: "I go to a dark place and cry. As a little girl, when I felt overwhelmed, I'd hide in a closet and just cry until I felt better. I didn't want my sister and older brother to see me cry. I wanted to be strong for them. The same in high school. For many years I'd do that almost every day. By the time I got to college, I cried far less and didn't always have a closet to crawl into. Now as a college-educated woman, I still cry, but rarely. The world is a brighter place for me now. Someday I pray and believe I won't need a dark place to cry."

RYAN

"My parents were not only imperfect, they were in a sense broken."

What does a normal family look like? In five-year-old Ryan's mind, it looked like his family. Because he was an only child, his parents were his whole world. But his schizophrenic father had moved out. And his mother battled bipolar disorder. Dysfunction junction, some might say. For Ryan, it was all he knew.

Ryan Winthrop was born in Cape Cod. By the time he started first grade, Ryan had lived in Maine, Tennessee, and Ohio. At least one of those moves was his mother's attempt at escaping his father. Ryan's father's mental illness required that he take medication. "The problem was when he didn't take it, he would get violent towards my mother. In Tennessee, he dragged my mother by her hair across the ground." His dad was like Dr. Jekyll and Mr. Hyde. Medicated, he was pleasant, wicked smart, humorous. Off his meds: dark, angry, volatile.

And then there was Ryan's mother's mental health to consider. "Several times a year my mother would check into a mental health facility to deal with her manic depression." As with Ryan's father, medication was prescribed to treat her condition. But she consistently self-medicated with alcohol. Vodka was her go-to coping mechanism. By middle school Ryan had a PhD in mental health—or so it felt. Not textbook knowledge, but hard-knocks wisdom, both emotional and physical. "I think mental illness is entirely complex, and a lot of the times there's a stigma against people with it. We ostracize people with it. It's a detriment. There are people who deny treatment because there is a stigma, and as a result people don't seek out help. They self-medicate, and people around them live in denial or become enablers." And there is perhaps at least another category: victim. For more years than he allows himself to consider, Ryan was a victim of his parents' mental illness. By the age of ten he was, by necessity, an old soul. He thought older, he behaved older, and because of the weight of his parents' demons, he felt older.

As a child, Ryan not only had the demands of coping with his parents' mental health problems, he also had the pressures that every kid has to deal with. "I didn't have a lot of friends. I was being bullied at that time." Undersized for his age, he was a frequent target of classmates. By his own admission, Ryan was an easy mark. "As an only child, I didn't have the social development I needed. As a result, when I was hanging out with other people, . . . I would cherish things that were trivial. Kids would touch my things and it upset me. I would get upset very easily. People associated me with being a crybaby and uncool. In general, I was not well liked."

He was isolated both at home and at school. His parents were overwhelmed with their own problems and couldn't provide much support. So Ryan was often left to fend for himself. School was a daily battlefield, and he was unable to defend himself or ask for help. "It took all the energy I had to survive mornings and evenings at home. I was exhausted by the time I got to school. Although most of the attention I got at school was negative, it was still attention."

Ryan came to see that the drama surrounding his family was a far cry from his peers' lives. "I was jealous of other families. I know there's no normal, but not to the extreme I had to deal with. I don't think I've fully come to accept that even to this day. I see other people and their parents, and it makes me envious. I know people have their own issues, but I admit [that] when I see a happy family, the green-eyed monster comes out."

By the time Ryan became a teenager, his parents were virtually divorced. He had been living with his mother. Ryan's father lived alone in an apartment. Ryan was now thirteen. Dealing with adolescence had its own challenges, but with his dad out of the house and his mother in a reasonable place, life was more pleasant than it had ever been. "I knew better than to think the lows were over."

None was lower than the day his father was discovered dead in his apartment.

"I remember this vividly. We hadn't heard from him for a few days. I was in my room with friends watching *The Breakfast Club*. We hear a loud knock at the door. Don't think much of it. My mom runs into the room and says, 'Your father is dead.' I froze. For a moment millions of thoughts rushed through my head. I never thought it would happen to my dad. We rushed to his place. You could feel the heavy weight of loss. I didn't breathe for a minute. I went to the living room, where the police were, and I started crying."

An odd thing happened next. No one stopped to console him. A young boy was crying in the room next to where his father's body lay, and no one took time to comfort him? It was symbolic of how Ryan had felt most his life: emotionally alone and responsible for his own well-being. So he did what he often did in stressful moments: He watched television. One evening while feeling particularly numb to his circumstance, he found himself watching *The Breakfast Club* again. He remembered the film's closing song, "Don't You (Forget About

Me).” It could have been his theme song at the time.

His dad was fifty-one. He died of chronic obstructive pulmonary disease.

A lot happened in Ryan’s life around that time that provided an impetus for change. “My middle school absorbed another middle school, and there was a whole new group of people in my life. I saw it as an opportunity. I put on another personality.”

But just as Ryan was putting himself together, his mother was falling apart.

When Ryan’s father was alive, he had been a big financial help to Ryan and his mother. Now that his father was gone, so was the money that he sent them. The financial strain took a toll on Ryan’s mom, who began once again to drown her sorrows in a bottle of vodka. Despite joining Alcoholics Anonymous and finding emotional support in the group, she tried to commit suicide six months later. Ryan was fourteen. “I had no idea what was going on until I heard a loud sound. I woke up to police banging at the door. Mom had called her sponsor, Ellen, while she was trying to kill herself. Ellen called the police, and they found her in the bathtub. She actually died while overdosing on meds and alcohol. They brought her back to life." A numbness had fallen over him since his father died. There were no tears this time. Ryan knew from past experience that no one was coming to rescue him. He looked for the positives: His mother might finally get the help she desperately needed.

"Mom was sent to a state hospital two hundred miles away, and I lived with my grandparents for three months." She was treated for her mental health issues and alcoholism, and returned home.

"We were okay until I was sixteen. That's when we had more financial issues, and she tried to commit suicide again. At that point my mom was dealing with a lot at work. She just got demoted. She took an assortment of sleeping medication because she wanted to sleep. She came into my room and told me that. We went to the hospital. I drove her. They pumped her stomach. It was one of those moments where I had to be the parent . . . where I had to make up for my mother's mistakes. This time I saved her life. After that suicide attempt we had a conversation about whether she should go back to the state hospital, and we agreed that she should."

At the age of sixteen, Ryan felt like he was forty-six. The strain of his mother's illness had taken a toll not only on him, but also on his grandparents. There was never a formal discussion, but Ryan knew he was now on his own. His grandparents had their lives to live. And he had a routine he knew he could manage. He went to school, had a job, and handled all of the responsibilities that most adults deal with—chores, food, and bills. "I was taking care of myself. It wasn't the worst-case scenario because I was getting social security and getting money from my job. I didn't want to go back to my grandparents because it was a major inconvenience on them." He wasn't entirely alone; his roommates were his two cats: Buttons and Sparkles.

"You always have options in life. Push forward or crumble. I decided to push forward. When I was in high school, dealing with everything that was going on, I was driven by the fact that other people thought I was impressive and that I stayed away from drugs and alcohol. I felt I was unique. I thought, *I'm forging a path for myself despite all of these circumstances. I'm one of a kind.* I wanted to be special."

On his seventeenth birthday Ryan visited his mom in the mental hospital. He came home to an empty house and ate a cupcake by himself to celebrate. "By now I was fully aware of my parents' limitations, [their] mental health issues, and the potential impact it might have on me. Might I be prone to some mental health problems? There are different schools of thought. One thing life with my parents taught me: If I was truly honest with myself, I could find help if and when the time [came]. I lost my sense of spirituality years ago, but if there is a God, I'll be spared the burden that seemed to cripple my parents. Meantime, I will make the choice to be optimistic."

When asked, "Where do you go, where do you hide, when the world hurts too much?" Ryan quickly names three places: "Video games, music, and theater." There is a measure of escapism in all three, but the one that set his life on the more positive of trajectories was theater. "I had a crush on a girl in school who was involved in theater. I figured, to get close to her, I had to get into theater. The relationship, if you want to call it that, didn't last. My love for theater has only grown." As did his love for school and a handful of teachers.

For Ryan, theater was far more than an escape; it gave him a place to be and lives to explore. He would often compare his circumstances to those of characters in plays. How would Ryan manage in their lives? How would they manage in his? It gave him the opportunity and space to step outside his circumstances and see life from a different angle. And the creative nature of theater gave him a constructive outlet to express his emotions, from anger and fear to joy and happiness. In theater it was okay to let his guard down.

"I had awesome teachers. People who cared. Who listened. I was driven. Because I lost my father, I didn't have a father figure. So in high school I gravitated to male teachers. Two in particular: my senior English teacher and my theater teacher. My English teacher was a kind man. He made me fall in love with English. I actually hated reading until I took his class. And I had my theater teacher for all four years. He was a father figure to me. He was kind of my dad through my high school years, whether he knew it or not. He provided me with structure while believing in me. I learned a lot of life lessons in theater. I learned how to express myself. . . . I think theater helped with that. It helped turn me from an introvert into an extrovert. Theater has been impactful, and I feel more alive when I'm involved in a production."

Ryan worked hard in high school and won several scholarships to help him pursue his goal of going to college. "My mother had been sober for a while, or so she had said, but I had a suspicion she was drinking again. So when I was to be presented some scholarships, I said I didn't want her to come along because she had been lying to me. I was kind of being a parent to my mom. And so later that night she tried to commit suicide one more time."

Once again finances were on his mother's mind. "We were facing being homeless. You see, when you graduate from high school, you lose your social security benefits. And my mom didn't have a job."

But Ryan didn't win just one or two scholarships. When all was said and done, he won a total of twenty-five scholarships. "I was able to not only pay for college, I was actually *paid* to go to college. And I was even able to loan my mom money to make sure she could cover her bills. And my mom is doing better." Just like Ryan found his passion in theater, his mom seemed to find her place in the world of social services. She now works with underprivileged teens. She helps them out in any way she can. "While my mom is not the most responsible, she is one of the kindest, most supportive women I know. Her mental health is pretty good. She seems happy."

Ryan graduated from a state university with a 3.94 GPA and a double major in English and theater. He had actually taken prelaw courses and decided it wasn't for him. So in the end he had gone back to his real passion: theater. He's now a tour actor and director with a children's theater. And like his high school mentor, he's teaching.

"I go to a new town across the US every week. I work with up to sixty-four kids a week. I teach, act, and direct. I teach them for a period of four or five days, and then we perform an hour-long musical at the end of the week. We perform it for the community." Ryan has taught over two thousand kids in just the past year.

His greatest asset as a teacher? "I think the big word here is 'empathy,'" says Ryan. "I've come across kids who are suicidal, on the verge of homelessness, and fighting for their lives. When a child acts out, I feel like I'm able to provide another perspective behind it and what they could potentially be going through. When I was a child, no one knew what I was going through and . . . why I was acting that way. I'm not perfect, but I hope I'm better able to do it than your average teacher."

As Ryan reflects back on his childhood, he doesn't have self-pity. Just the opposite. "I do think I'm fortunate in that fact. I'm lucky. I get to have this perspective. When I won the scholarships, I told my mom, 'Thank you for not giving me the best life. It helped make me the person I am today. I learned to take care of myself and to be self-sufficient.'"

Ryan dreams big. The twenty-three-year-old is mulling over a future as an actor in Hollywood. "My life goals have changed in the past few years. It would be amazing if I could go into acting or theater. I now know the importance of being able to take risks and achieve in uncomfortable situations. I'm now finding a balance. I think I'm now trying to find a balance in life that is stable. I tell myself, 'It's okay to take risks. It's okay to be out there. You are going to bounce back. You're going to be okay. If you fail, it's okay. Life turns out okay.'"

Ryan has even been dabbling with the stock market. "I kind of like it. Do you know, five years ago around this time, my mom and I were living with one dollar in the bank? I've been able to save up money. I've invested in a mutual fund, and I have a healthy savings account. I'm able to fortify myself a bit and let life take me where it takes me. Maybe I'll try my hand at Hollywood . . . and I'll see where life takes me . . . if it doesn't work, at least I tried."

But beyond his professional dreams is one goal he knows for sure. He wants a family. A healthy family.

Where do you go, where do you hide, when the world hurts too much? For Ryan the answer is: "The arts [theater and music]. They allow me the space to escape but also surround myself with joy. The sound of music brings me joy. The chance to perform and create in theater brings me joy. When I'm hurting, the arts can heal me. Give me strength for the next obstacle to come."

TYTON

"When my brother was murdered, part of me died."

We've all had bad days. Tyton Charles had a bad year. It was like one long tidal wave of heartbreak after heartbreak. A drunk driver killed his beloved older brother. His mother and stepfather divorced. He was diagnosed with juvenile diabetes. He was twelve. "I thought I'd fallen into a hole I'd never climb out of," Tyton says.

Tyton Charles is from Lafayette, Louisiana. He's the youngest of Felicia Carmouche's three children.

"My mother is my hero. I've watched her go without food so her children could eat. She's fiercely loyal. A real warrior when it comes to her children. My greatest champion, for sure."

It's worth noting Tyton's description of his mother; there is also a connection between war and his very name. "Perhaps the biggest thing my father ever gave me was my name. He's a fan of Greek mythology. He liked the idea Titans were powerful. It took me a long time to realize I, too, am powerful." Tyton says it took adversity for him to find how strong he could be.

By middle school the person in Tyton's life who was closest to a Greek god was his older brother, Dontrell. The two were inseparable. Dontrell was both protector and best friend. While many older siblings shy away from younger brothers and sisters, Dontrell loved having Tyton around. Tyton thought his big brother was invincible. Until the day he wasn't.

"I remember the day my brother died. He was driving with a friend and texting at the same time. He dropped his phone and reached to pick it up. That's when a drunk driver crossed over into his lane. My brother's car flipped over. He died instantly. His friend survived."

It was the first time Tyton had seen his mother cry or heard her scream. He felt paralyzed. For days he held on to the belief there'd been a mistake. His hero would walk through the door again. By the morning of the funeral it was time to accept reality. It was the worst pain he'd ever felt. There were even moments he wished he'd been the one who died. Now that his big brother was dead, who'd protect him? Soon enough much of his pain was replaced with anger. He was angry at his loss and even angrier that many of the adults in his life had moved on. As time passed, relatives talked less and less about his brother.

"The driver was convicted and spent some time in prison. We lost track of him and my brother's friend. I guess it was easier for all of them and eventually me to just move on. Our family was devastated by his loss. I'm not sure you ever recover. 'Closure' is a nice word, but I'm not sure what it means. Not a day passes I don't think about him. My brother was eighteen years old, six years older than me. I never knew a person's heart could hurt so much. As sad as I was, I think it was far worse for my mother. You could see it in her eyes, in the way she dragged herself around. She put on a good face for the rest of the family as often as she could, but more than a few times I heard her crying in her room. All these years later we're still grieving. My brother was my hero. My go-to guy. I was angry at the world. How could such a good person be taken away? I guess that's a question most people ask when they lose a loved one. I wish I knew a good answer."

Losing a loved one is never easy, but Tyton's loss was compounded by his mother's financial difficulties and failing marriage, and his declining health. For years Tyton's stepfather had been the closest thing he'd ever had to a father actively involved in his life. His real father and mother never married.

"My dad and I have never been close. My stepdad is the only real dad I've ever known. He loved and provided for our family. I've never been certain of the details, but my parents' marriage slowly fell apart. I guess every divorce is difficult. My mom and stepdad's was no different. When they split, my mom had to go back to work full-time. That alone was a tough transition. The separation and eventual divorce would strain my relationship with him, but years later, by the time I finished high school, we'd sorted things out. He was invited to my graduation. I'm glad he was there."

That reconciliation would be years in the making, but back in middle school it seemed as though the world around Tyton was crumbling, as was his own health. Still mourning the loss of his brother, with his mother's financial troubles becoming more apparent, Tyton was hit with another unexpected blow: He was diagnosed with juvenile diabetes. There is an old Christian saying: "God doesn't put heavy burdens on weak shoulders." Tyton wondered if God thought he was a triplet. Family trauma drained him emotionally. Diabetes tugged at him emotionally, spiritually, physically, and academically. "Not long after the diagnosis my grades began to fall. When my sugar level was high, I was easily agitated. Difficult to be around, I would fall into a deep funk or an angry rage. If my sugar level was low, I could pass out just as easily. It took some time for us to find the right dose of insulin to even things out. The drug began to work much faster than the rest of my life."

For Tyton, the best part of middle school was graduating. "As soon as I got to high school, everything started to change. I poured myself into school. Freshman year represented a fresh start. Most of the friends I had in middle school had grown very distant quickly after my brother's death and my health issues. I must admit I wasn't the easiest person to like in middle school. I really only had two friends: my mom and my late brother, Dontrell. Though he was no longer with me physically, I felt his spirit inside me. He was still watching over me. It was as if he was telling me it was now okay to move on. And move I did."

And it was liberating. Tyton realized he couldn't change the past. The facts were the facts. He discovered that all he had was today and maybe tomorrow. His brother's death was a constant reminder that tomorrow wasn't promised, so he'd better go for what he wanted today. So he did.

"I became freshman class president, joined the soccer team, my grades were on the rise again, and very soon I found something I was passionate about. Actually, two things I became passionate about: art and music. I now had a reason to live and feel good about life. There was light to shine in the dark places of my soul. It also helped that I began to see my mother in a different way: no longer just a victim of her circumstances, but a real fighter. She started her own business. With financial stability came a strength that spread to the rest of our family. I'm so proud of her."

When asked where he would go, where he would hide, when the world hurt too much, Tyton's initial response is a "quiet place where I [could] be alone." But he quickly filled that quiet place with the sound of music. "Music gives me a place to escape to, and once there, I love to write, to draw, to express myself," he says. "And so I discovered I was also good at it. Friends liked the things I could create. Some friends told me my gift helped them. In learning I could help people, I learned to help myself. That ability to change someone else (through my music or art) helped me change myself. I also discovered I wasn't the only person who felt alone. I wasn't the only person hurting. Everyone experiences hurt. It's how you learn to deal with it that separates success from failure. From the lyrics to a rap, writing poetry, or one of my drawings I found something that I was not only good at, but also deeply enjoyed. I'd found my passion. And by doing so, I found the source of my joy. For the longest time after my brother's death I was looking for someone or something to replace him. There is no replacing him. But I have managed to fill the rest of life with good people, good activities, that all give me purpose."

By his senior year in high school Tyton had won several scholarships and had many options for college. He chose Louisiana State University in Baton Rogue. He has a Southern sensibility, so going to college in his beloved state of Louisiana was an easy choice. LSU is not far from home, but far enough. His mom can visit, but she will almost certainly have to call first. As he did the transition from middle school to high school, Tyton sees going off to college as liberating. He can take the lessons learned and talents developed in high school with him to Baton Rouge.

It's also the opportunity to hit the reset button on

parts of himself he'd like to let go of. Mixed with the nervousness that goes with the unknown, he also feels a great sense of pride. "I'm only the second person in my family to go to college. My mother's education was sidetracked when she had her first child at eighteen. My remaining older brother went into the army, and after an honorable discharge he went to work in construction. College isn't for everyone. I get that. College doesn't guarantee a job or success, but it's the right path for me."

He's decided to major in animation. His dream job after college is to work for Marvel Comics. He's loved comic books for as long as he can remember. "Maybe I'll work on the next *Spider-Man*. I know it's a wild dream. But dreams beat nightmares. I've had plenty of those in my life. Nightmares I let go of. Dreams I hold on to."

Where do you go, where do you hide, when the world hurts too much? For Tyton the answer is: "The creative part of my soul. I love to create music and sketches. I'm good at it. It makes me happy. When I'm in the creative process, I can feel as strong as a Greek god."

NOTES

At the time of this writing all the young people written about in this book are in a good place or well on their way. Perhaps Tania has always been the most vulnerable: a young woman of color from an impoverished background with more than her share of emotional scars. She started farthest behind and thus had the most ground to make up. For all of them there is likely no fairy-tale ending. There will be challenges to come, obstacles to overcome. One of the powerful lessons they taught me, at least, is that it's not so much the outcome in life that matters most, it is the effort. Controlling what one can control and doing one's best to let go of the rest. My late mother, Clarice Pitts, would always put it this way: "Let go and let God." It's a familiar take on the Scripture found in Romans 8:28: "All things work together for good to those who love God, those who are called according to his purpose." For Mason, Pappy, Michaela, Ryan, Tyton, and yes, Tania, there is a calling. They all seem to hear it above the screams of their pasts and day-to-day circumstances. They have chosen to be the one.

Where do you go, where do you hide, when the world hurts too much? Hopefully, you have a place. These outstanding young people have all found a safe place, a constructive place. Some are physical locations, others are emotional, many are psychological. These young people you've met are certainly exceptional for what they've achieved. They made this book because of what they've overcome. I pray there is a little of them in all of us, in you. If you haven't found it yet, keep looking. Stay forever optimistic.

* * *

A special thanks goes to the Horatio Alger Association in Washington, DC. They stand in the gap for young people like many of those mentioned in this book, by providing financial and emotional support in college. The association offers millions of dollars in college scholarships to students who've been dealt a tough hand. Members believe adversity doesn't have to break people, it can help build them. And with help those same young people can make the world better for future generations.

My continued gratitude goes to the great team at Dupree/Miller in Dallas, Texas. In particular, Jan Miller and Nena Madonia for their good counsel and enduring friendship. To my editor, Justin Chanda, whose clear vision and steady hand helped guide this project. And to my ABC News family, who give me the opportunity to see the world and meet many of God's best children, some living in desperate situations. Those children remind me that each day we are allowed breath, we have a chance, no matter the circumstances we face. A chance to make our future better than our past.

RESOURCES

All of the incredible individuals you read about in this book overcame significant challenges. What you'll notice as a connecting thread across the stories is that they didn't do this alone. If you're struggling too, there are places you can go for help.

Crisis Text Line

A free 24/7 support for those in crisis. Text 741741 from anywhere in the USA to text with a trained Crisis Counselor. The counselors are there to help you stay safe and healthy.

Mental Health & Substance Abuse Services Finder
(findtreatment.samhsa.gov)

A confidential and anonymous resource that will help you find treatment facilities in the United States or US Territories for substance abuse/addiction and/or mental health problems.

StopBullying.gov

A comprehensive website with tools for preventing, stopping, and addressing bullying in a variety of contexts.

Just as reading *this* book has probably opened your mind to new ways of seeing and understanding, young adult (YA) literature—that is, books written expressly for teenagers that dignify teenage lives and concerns—may also have a special usefulness and power.

As longtime YA critic Patty Campbell maintains, the best young adult novels explore a fundamental human question: "Who am I, and what am I going to do about it?" With this question, these novels locate teens' experiences in a larger context where reflection can give rise to action.

The following YA novels depict teenagers in various forms of crisis who find hope and strength as they explore their identities and question injustice:

We Were Here by Matt de la Peña
(Delacorte, 2009)
Three California teens run away from a group home in search of new lives and some sense of belonging in a world that would just as soon reduce them to their crimes. For main character Miguel, recovery from trauma becomes possible through reading, writing, and discovering shared humanity with others.

Sorta Like a Rock Star by Matthew Quick
(Little, Brown, 2010)
Living in an abandoned school bus with her alcoholic mother doesn't deter Amber Appleton from her mission to spread hope in the community. Then she suffers an unthinkable tragedy. Counseling meetings with her Korean priest and haikus written by a reclusive army veteran assist her in regaining hope and finding a path toward healing.

***American Street* by Ibi Zoboi**
(HarperCollins, 2017)
Haitian teenager Fabiola Toussaint's hopes for a new life in America are dashed when her mother is detained in customs at Newark Airport. Her only choice is to continue on to Detroit and build a life with her aunt and cousins. In the process, she struggles to navigate moral dilemmas and dangers in an unforgiving world.

This list was compiled by the National Council of Teachers of English (NCTE), and the book recommendations provided by NCTE member Jennifer Buehler, associate professor at Saint Louis University and author of *Teaching Reading with YA Literature: Complex Texts, Complex Lives*, a publication of the National Council of Teachers of English.